# WANTED:
## THE WORLD

**Wanted: The World**
**The Well-Meant Offer of the Gospel from a Missionary's Perspective**

Text copyright © 2016 Sovereign Grace Missionary Press

ISBN: 978-0-9983187-0-7 (POD)

Scripture quotations from The Authorized (King James) Version. Rights in the Authorized Version in the United Kingdom are vested in the Crown. Reproduced by permission of the Crown's patentee, Cambridge University Press.

Cover photo: gracerankin photography ©
Publishing and Design Services: MelindaMartin.me

# WANTED:
## THE WORLD

### THE WELL-MEANT OFFER
### OF THE GOSPEL FROM A
### MISSIONARY'S PERSPECTIVE

## TREVOR JOHNSON
### WITH GRACE RANKIN

Sovereign Grace Missionary Press

# CONTENTS

"Ho, every one that thirsteth, come ye to the waters, and he that hath no money; come ye, buy, and eat; yea, come, buy wine and milk without money and without price."

—Isaiah 55:1

# PREFACE

"Do you REALLY believe God wants to save ME?"

The man who stood before me spoke very slowly, his words struggling out from under the deep weight of his sins. Their toll was heavy and he was now a "very old" young man, his care-worn face and sagging shoulders displaying the deep torment upon him.

He knew his own propensity to fall short despite his occasional desires for salvation. He had heard the gospel invitation many times before. He now heard it again from me. But the good news did not seem good, nor did it bring joy or relief to his face—only a sense of worry and anxiety. Were his sins too many? Had he sinned away his day of grace? Would God still accept him?

*"Do you really believe God wants to save even me?"* he asked again.

How should I respond?

As a good Calvinist who believes in the predestination of God's elect to salvation, should I respond in a noncommittal manner? Should I exercise caution so I don't stir up false hopes—hopes that belong to God's elect sheep alone—in a possible reprobate? Should I be careful not to offer the love of God too broadly? Should I refrain from speaking of God's love for fear that God actually hates this man and desires his damnation? Could it be that I might offer God's grace more openly than He would have me do?

I could respond, *"Maybe God loves you...if you show repentance."* Or, *"Perhaps this gospel invitation is for you...but we can't be sure! Try to exercise conviction of sin and faith so that I can know if I may extend this gracious offer to you."* Or perhaps, *"Maybe God loves you and maybe God desires your good...or He could hate you...I just don't know His will."*

Or I could simply answer, *"Yes! Yes. God cares for you and desires your salvation."* I could assure him that, *"Yes, God desires to save you and would do it even today due to His great love!"*

But is this right?

# INTRODUCTION

I am a missionary to a remote Papuan tribe. I am also fully predestinarian—I believe in the election of certain people to salvation. I believe that God is sovereign in all things including salvation. I believe that all events great and small throughout all of history fall out according to His predestinating purposes.

I affirm that, *"God, from all eternity, by the most wise and holy counsel of His will, freely and unchangeably ordained whatever comes to pass."*

I affirm that the number of the elect—those chosen for salvation—is fixed and unchangeable from all eternity and that, *"These angels and men, thus predestinated and foreordained, are particularly and unchangeably designed, and their number so certain and definite, that it cannot be either increased or diminished."*

I also affirm, however, that God loves all of mankind and wishes them to be saved. I heartily echo John Calvin's comments on John 3:16: "…so we must see whence Christ came to us, and why he was offered to be our Savior…that Christ brought life, because the Heavenly Father loves the human race, and wishes that they should not perish" (Calvin). Furthermore, I pronounce a hearty amen over Matthew Henry's comments: "Though many of the world of mankind perish, yet God's giving his only-begotten Son was an instance of his love to the whole world, because through him there is a *general offer* of life and salvation made to all" (1540).

God loves and sincerely desires the salvation of all men and graciously offers the gospel to each one, sending many kind invitations. These summons are not merely addressed to the elect only, but to all. His general gospel call goes out to the entire world, to every person in it. And the impetus for this kind offer of the gospel is His gracious and sincere love for His creation.

That unbelievers do not benefit from Christ's death is due to their own sin, not to any narrowness on God's part. "Men evangelized cannot go to hell but over the bowels of God's great mercies. They must wade to it through the blood of Christ, and trample that blood under foot" (Duncan).

## GOALS

In this book, I want to focus on five simple yet profound truths:

(1) This gospel offer is sufficient to save all and is offered to all.

(2) It is not merely a "free offer" or a cold command, but a sincere invitation borne out of God's loving disposition to bless all of His creatures.

(3) This gracious invitation reveals God's heart for His creation; He loves the world and desires its salvation.

(4) This kind disposition of God to bless His creatures fuels our desire to see the whole world blessed. We mirror the heart of God when we desire the salvation of the lost.

And finally,

(5) If we do not believe these truths, our passion for missions may suffer and we may grow cold toward the lost.

A firm belief in the well-meant and sincere offer of the gospel is vital to understanding the benevolent nature of our loving God and to fueling our missionary zeal for the souls of every person around us.

# 1

The gospel offer is sufficient to save all
and is offered to all.

We must emphatically declare that there is no lack of power in the atonement to save all mankind. Christ's death was sufficient to rescue the whole world. This is not my opinion alone, nor is it a modern sentiment, but is supported by Scripture and by documents of the historic Reformed faith.

In the book of Acts, the apostle Luke writes, "And the times of this ignorance God winked at [or overlooked]; but now commandeth *all men every where* to repent" (*The Holy Bible, King James Version,* Acts 17:30, emphasis added). The gospel is clearly, simply, and beautifully offered to every person.

The historic Reformed faith, even the most thoroughly Calvinistic Canons of Dort, also defends this view of the gospel's sufficiency and God's generosity in its second main point of doctrine (article 3), which declares: "This death of God's Son is the only and entirely complete sacrifice and satisfaction for sins; it is of infinite value and worth, more than sufficient to atone for the sins of the whole world" (126).

Christ's work on the cross is sufficient to save all. Not only that, but also this good news must go forth to all. Article 5 of Dort stresses our mandate to proclaim it to the world and every person in it: "Moreover, it is the promise of the gospel that whoever believes in Christ crucified shall not perish but have eternal life. This promise, together with the command to repent and believe, ought to be announced and declared without differentiation or discrimination to all nations and people, to whom God in his good pleasure sends the gospel" (127).

When offering salvation to someone, we do not need to worry whether Christ died for that particular person or not. We should not shrink from pleading for any sinner. We may beg each and every one without exception, *"Receive Christ and partake of Him!"* We do not need to fear offering anything that was not promised.

As John Owen has said, "There are none called by the gospel even once to enquire after the purpose and intention of God concerning the particular object of the death of Christ, everyone being fully assured that His death shall be profitable to them that believe in him and obey him" (Ellis). We are to offer Christ in an indiscriminate and unlimited manner to all.

When Jesus said to the crowds in John 5:34, "…but these things I say, that ye might be saved", He did not so demarcate the mass as to divide them into two camps (*"that you, but not you, may be saved"*). Instead He spoke generally, presenting an invitation to all. None in that crowd needed to worry whether or not Christ would have accepted him if he desired salvation.

Some may call it inconsistent that God offers the gospel to all and yet provides atonement for only the elect. In his book, *Calvinism: Pure and Mixed,* W.G.T. Shedd addresses this concern:

> Confession vii.3, declares that "man by his fall having made himself incapable of life by that (legal) covenant, the Lord was pleased to make a second, commonly called the covenant of grace: wherein he freely offered to sinners life and salvation by Jesus Christ, requiring of them faith in him, that they may be saved, and promising to give unto all those that are ordained unto life, his Holy Spirit, to make them willing and able to believe." Two distinct and different things are mentioned here: (a) an offer of salvation; (b) a promise of the Holy Spirit to make the unwilling sinner willing to accept it. The number of those to whom the offer of salvation is made is unlimited; of those to whom the promise of the Spirit to "make them willing" is made, is limited by "ordination to life" or election. It is clear that God may desire that to be done by man under the influence of his common grace in the common call, which he may not decide and purpose to *make* him do by the operation of his special grace in the effectual call. His desire that sinners would hear his universal call to repentance may be, and is unlimited; but his purpose to overcome their unwillingness and incline them to repentance may be, and is limited.

God offers Christ's sacrifice to every man, without exception, and assures him that if he will trust in it he shall be saved, and gives him common grace to help and encourage him to believe. This is a proof that God loves his soul and desires its salvation. But God does not, in addition to this universal offer of mercy, promise to overcome every man's aversion to believe and repent and his resistance of common grace. Election and preterition have no reference to the offer of salvation or to common grace. They relate only to special grace and the effectual application of Christ's sacrifice. The universal offer of mercy taught in this section evinces the universality of God's compassion towards sinners. (28-29)

In Revelation 22, we read, "And the Spirit and the bride say, Come. And let him that heareth say, Come. And let him that is athirst come. And whosoever will, let him take the water of life freely" (Rev. 22:17). God's Holy Spirit and God's Holy Church, His bride, both give an unrestricted invitation: *"Come."*

# 2

This gospel offer is not merely a "free offer" or a cold command, but a sincere invitation borne out of God's loving disposition to bless all of His creatures.

Strangely enough, I have met some Calvinists who, though they do not balk at the language of the "free offer", will not permit themselves to say that it is also a *"well-meant"* and *"sincere"* one. In their view, we may offer the good news, but we should not say that God actually wants all people to take Him up on it. So they assert that the language of a "free offer" is permissible, but any mention of a *"sincere, well-meant offer"* is verboten and equates to some form of incipient Arminianism.

No!

The gospel is an invitation originating in the gracious bosom of God. His heart is in it! The very definition of *offer* is to demonstrate one's intentions toward another. The sincerity is assumed lest we feel compelled to qualify it as a mock offer or deception. And what is more evil than to offer life to a dying man and not truly mean it?

J.I. Packer says it well: "God in the gospel expresses a bona fide wish that all may hear, and that all who hear may believe and be saved" (151).

When God proclaims, "Look unto me, and be ye saved, all the ends of the earth; for I *am* God, and *there is* none else" (Isa. 45:22), are we to doubt that He is sincere in this appeal? Wouldn't we take it at face value that God desires it?

2 Corinthians 5:20 tells us, "Now then we are ambassadors for Christ, as though God did beseech *you* by us: we pray *you* in Christ's stead, be ye reconciled to God". If we as Christ's ambassadors plead with sinners, "*be ye reconciled to God*", and if this action is likened to God Himself pleading with sinners through us, why would we doubt Him to be sincere? The plain reading of this text makes it clear that God means it.

The Westminster Divine Jeremiah Burroughs confirms that when preachers beseech sinners to be saved, it is actually "…the beseechings and entreatings of God himself…God begs of thee to come in…" (216-217).

Others speak of God kneeling to entreat sinners, and even state that He *"goeth a-begging"* for lost souls. Men devoted to the doctrine of divine election and opposed to Arminianism made these statements.

If Jesus wept as He approached Jerusalem (Luke 19) and wished that the children of Israel would be gathered to Him in such a tender fashion as a mother hen gathering her chicks (Matthew 23), are we to suppose these to be crocodile tears which flowed down the cheeks of our Savior? Was this some sham mourning? Should we dismiss it as weakness in Christ's human nature or activity in His human emotions that is wholly incongruent with His divinity? Was it not the whole Person of Christ who wept in His perfect example to man?

Furthermore, is it a mock grief by God when He laments, "Oh that my people had hearkened unto me, *and* Israel had walked in my ways" (Psalm 81:13)? Do we empty this of all meaningful content by confining it to the level of mere anthropopathism—ascribing human feelings and emotions to a non-human being—and deny God's sincerity in these statements? After all, it is the Holy Spirit who inspired these specific phrases of mourning and revealed every word so man might know the nature of God.

In fact, God reveals that He actually desired Israel's obedience. As Richard Alleine so passionately puts it, "Thy God did not mock thee, when he preached peace to thee; he was willing and wish'd it thine; if thou wouldst, thou mightest have made it thine own; but whilest he would thou wouldest not".

Dutch theologian Louis Berkhof writes this of the sincerity of God in the general call:

> It is a bona fide [good faith] calling. The external calling is a calling in good faith, a calling that is seriously meant. It is not an invitation coupled with the hope that it will not be accepted. When God calls the sinner to accept Christ by faith, He earnestly desires this; and when He promises those who repent and believe eternal life, His promise is dependable. This follows from the very nature, from the veracity, of God. It

is blasphemous to think that God would be guilty of equivocation and deception, that He would say one thing and mean another, that He would earnestly plead with the sinner to repent and believe unto salvation, and at the same time not desire it in any sense of the word. The bona fide character of the external call is proved by the following passages of Scripture: Num. 23:19; Ps. 81:13-16; Prov. 1:24; Isa. 1:18-20; Ezek. 18:23, 32; 33:11; Matt. 21:37; 2 Tim. 2:13. The Canons of Dort also assert it explicitly in [sections] 3 and 4.8. (397-398)

It is not enough merely to speak of God's "free offer" of salvation—it is also a genuine and honest one.

In Matthew 22:1-14, we see God's kingdom of heaven compared to a great marriage feast. Runners were sent to carry the invitation to all—an invitation that did not bear on its seal, "For the elect only." No distinction was made; God sincerely entreated all: "Behold, I have prepared my dinner: my oxen and *my* fatlings *are* killed, and all things *are* ready: come unto the marriage" (Matt. 22:4). The reason many would not come was not that the call lacked fervency, for the invitations went out vigorously. It was not that the King was not gracious; His arms were held wide open. It was that the invited ones were unwilling to come, and they offered up stupid excuses to the detriment of their souls.

In his sermon "Gospel Presentations are the Strongest Invitations", Puritan James Durham says, "God the Father, and the King's Son the Bridegroom, are not only content and willing, but very desirous to have sinners come to the marriage. They would fain (to speak with reverence) have poor souls espoused to Christ" (44).

With men it is unseemly but possible for the host of a feast to invite and yet not desire the presence of his guests, and even to lie about his pleasure at their attendance. Yet we should not attribute this weakness to God. In Matthew 22, there is a stated desire on the part of the Host to have His house full! Who is that Host anyway? And what does this parable teach of His disposition toward sinners? Even when there was a guest discovered who did not wear the right wedding garment, the Host still tenderly called him "friend", and the ejection of this guest was not due in any part to him coming uninvited, but due to his lack of proper attire—he was invited and desired, yet not clothed in the righteousness of Christ.

Are we to suppose that God offers salvation using terms that describe His lovingkindness, yet isn't really sincere? Are His parables misleading or do they tell of His inviting nature? Does God offer Christ and then not truly desire sinners to take hold of Him? Does God paint pictures of an inviting Host when He actually does not desire that all should come?

*The Sum of Saving Knowledge* by the aforementioned James Durham and David Dickson shows its high place in the eyes of many of the Reformed, as it is often published alongside editions of the *Westminster Confession of Faith*. Take a look at how it describes the gospel offer:

> He that, upon the loving request of God and Christ, made to him by the mouth of ministers, (having commission to that effect,) hath embraced the offer of perpetual reconciliation through Christ, and doth purpose, by God's grace, as a reconciled person, to strive against sin, and to serve God to his power constantly, may be as sure to have righteousness and eternal life given to him, for the obedience of Christ imputed to him, as it is sure that Christ was condemned and put to death for the sins of the redeemed imputed to him... (Dickson)

It continues, "...if any man shall not be taken with the sweet invitation of God, nor with the humble and loving request of God, made to him to be reconciled, he shall find he hath to do with the sovereign authority of the highest Majesty..." (Dickson).

This most sound and respected document of the Reformed faith, therefore, refers to the gospel offer as *"the loving request of God"*, *"the sweet invitation of God"*, and *"the humble and loving request"* of God. This is no language of mere cold command! It speaks of God's sincere desire to bless.

# GOD NOT ONLY INVITES, BUT ALSO PLEADS AND BEGS

Many staid Calvinists scoff at sermon illustrations depicting God knocking at the door of the sinner's heart. *"God begs no man!"* they will thunder. *"God commands, but He never begs!"*

But the reader will be surprised to know that there is a long history of Calvinistic writers speaking of God *"begging"* the sinner to believe, even using such phrases as *"kneeling"* or *"on bended knee"*.

Stephen Charnock's words sound almost shocking to many Calvinists who have reacted so vigorously to Arminians and desire to give them not an inch of ground. He writes that the appeal of the minister of the gospel is, "…as if Divine goodness did kneel down to a sinner with ringed hands and blubbered cheeks…". This Calvinistic writer pictures God Himself kneeling with *"blubbered cheeks"* on behalf of the sinner out of love!

Thomas Boston's depiction of God's sincere desire to save is not out of the ordinary at all:

> Many do not consider, nor believe that Christ is knocking at the door of their hearts for admission, and therefore they do not bestir themselves to receive him. But believe it, it is no fancy, but the most certain reality, and therefore I say to you and to each of you: "To you is the word of this salvation sent."…Christ is willing to come into every heart. Why does he demand open doors,

but because he is willing to enter? Though
the house be not worthy of his presence,
though he has received many indignities
from it and in it, yet he is willing to grace it
with his royal presence... See the glory of his
willingness to save! His whole word is full
of demonstrations of this. (97, 102-103, 106)

There is no reason to sacrifice the lovingkindness of
God or to minimize His kind entreaties in an effort to
magnify His sovereignty. The sovereign God is a loving
God whose disposition is to bless His creation.

## THIS DOCTRINE IS NOT A NEW ABNORMALITY, BUT HAS ALWAYS BEEN PART OF THE REFORMED FAITH

The belief in the sincerity of God in His offers of
mercy has a long history and is well represented by a
worthy crowd of theologians. We will explore fourteen
in particular here.

First, Martin Luther writes in his *Bondage of the
Will*: "For He desires that all men should be saved, in
that He comes to all by the word of salvation, and the
fault is in the will which does not receive Him; as He
says in Matt. 23: 'How often would I have gathered thy
children together, and thou wouldst not!'" (171)

A second Reformer, Martin Bucer, contends,
"According to His nature, God does good abundantly
and wishes to make every man blessed (1 Tim. 2:4)".

Third is *The First Helvetic Confession*, one of the first such documents of the Reformation era (and the first of national authority), which directly states, "The principle intent of all canonical Scripture is that God wishes to be good to mankind, and that He has declared that benevolence through Christ, His only Son" (Bullinger).

Fourth, we have the writings of Thomas Boston, which abound with mentions of God's sincere desire for the salvation of all men:

> Sinners are desired to come in. They not only have leave to come in, but they are desired by the Master of the house to come in. Arise then, ye worst of sinners, the "Master calleth you." Ye are called, not to a funeral, but a feast; not to a prison, but to the guest-chamber, where he may entertain you with all the delicacies of heaven. If ye were not desired, why would he send his servants to compel you to come in? and will ye refuse when ye are desired?

Fifth, the great preacher Charles Spurgeon said this of the genuineness of God's offer of life:

> Lost sinners who sit under the sound of the gospel are not lost for the want of the most affectionate invitation. God says he stretches out his hands....What did he wish them to come for? Why, to be saved. "No," says one, "it was for temporal mercies." Not

so, my friend; the verse before is concerning spiritual mercies. Now, was God sincere in his offer? God forgive the man who dares to say he was not. God is undoubtedly sincere in every act he did. He sent his prophets, he entreated the people of Israel to lay hold on spiritual things, but they would not, and though he stretched out his hands all the day long, yet they were "a disobedient and gainsaying people" and would not have his love. (341)

Sixth, the Puritan John Flavel writes:

The Redeemer's tears wept over obstinate Jerusalem, spake the zeal and fervency of his affection to their salvation; how loth Christ is to give up sinners. What a mournful voice is that in John 5:40, "And you will not come unto me, that you might have life." How fain would I give you life? but you would rather die than come unto me for it. What can Christ do more to express his willingness?

And seventh, Thomas Manton, in his sermon on John 3:16, states that there was no cause in us to bring about God's love: "No worthiness in us; for when his love moved Him to give Christ for us, He had all mankind in his prospect and view, as lying in the polluted mass, or in a state of sin and misery, and then provided a Redeemer for them".

J.C. Ryle, eighth, writes this rather striking estimation of Manton:

> Manton held strongly the doctrine of election. But that did not prevent him teaching that God loves all, and that His tender mercies are over all His works. He that wishes to see this truth set forth should read his sermon on the words, "God so loved the world that He gave His only-begotten Son" (John 3:16), and mark how he speaks of the world.

And ninth, Jonathan Edwards in his sermon, "Misery of the Damned" (1726), affirms that the offer of the gospel is God's sincere desire and pleadings to the unsaved to close with Christ: "And all this will be aggravated by the remembrance, that God once loved us so as to give his Son to bring us to the happiness of his love, and tried all manner of means to persuade us to accept of his favor, which was obstinately refused".

As the tenth example, we have John Collinges's words in *A Commentary on the Holy Bible by Matthew Poole*. His treatment of 1 Tim. 2:4 states:

> The apostle produces a clear, convincing reason, that the duty of charity in praying for all men is pleasing to God, from his love extended to all, in his willing their salvation, and their knowledge and belief of the gospel, which is the only way of salvation.

From hence our Savior's commission and command to the apostles was universal: Go and teach all nations, Matthew 28:19; Preach the gospel to every creature, that is, to every man, Mark 16:15; He excludes no people, no person.

Eleventh, the theologian R.B. Kuiper writes:

…Reformed theology describes the universal offer of salvation as sincere…God Himself, who has determined from eternity who are to be saved and who are not, and therefore distinguishes infallibly between the elect whom He designed to save by the death of Christ and the reprobate whom He did not design to save, makes on the ground of the universally suitable and sufficient atonement a most sincere, *bona fide*, offer of eternal life, not only to the elect but to all men, urgently invites them to life everlasting, and expresses the ardent desire that every person to whom this offer and this invitation come accept the offer and comply with the invitation.

We have already quoted from *The Canons of Dort*, the Calvinistic document of the Reformation era, which agrees perfectly with us on these points. For the twelfth example, we examine *A Puritan Theology*, "The Puritans on Coming to Christ", in which Joel Beeke, a modern reformed pastor and author, sums up Dort's position this way:

> ...The invitation does not lie or deceive; it is a true, rich, full, free invitation. The gospel is a well-meant offer. Christ has declared Himself ready and willing to receive all who to come to Him and to save them ... The call is based on the condition of faith, but it is a true invitation ... Judgment day will confirm this truth. No one will stand before God on the last day and say ... "I received the invitation, but I did not think it was sincere." The call to come to Christ is a well-meant offer of salvation addressed to every human being.

As the thirteenth example, we observe the great commentator Mathew Henry, whose annotations are replete with phrases that testify to his belief in this doctrine, such as this one in his words on Deuteronomy 5:29: "The God of heaven is truly and earnestly desirous of the welfare and salvation of poor sinners...he has no pleasure in the ruin of sinners" (192).

Our fourteenth and final point comes from a modern Reformed Baptist minister, Erroll Hulse, who writes, "The will of God is expressed in unmistakable terms". He further says, "He has no pleasure in the destruction and punishment of the wicked" (Ez. 18:32; 33:11). Hulse also cites Matthew 23:37, where Jesus weeps over the city of Jerusalem: "We are left in no doubt that the desire and will of God is for man's highest good, that is his eternal salvation through heeding the gospel of Christ" (21-22).

Speaking directly to this topic of the sincere free offer of the gospel in his article on John 3:16 and Hyper-Calvinism, Hulse writes further:

> By selective use of Reformed Confessions it is possible to claim to be reformed but at the same time hide the fact that you are a hyper-Calvinist. The hyper-Calvinist denies that God loves all mankind and that the gospel is good news to be declared to all without exception. That is the very essence of hyper-Calvinism. Calvin, the great organiser of the evangelisation of France, writes on John 3:16: 'For although there is nothing in the world deserving God's favour, he nevertheless shows he is favourable to the whole world when he calls all without exception to the faith of Christ.

And here is Hulse once more in "The Example of the English Puritans", showing that the modern Reformed Baptist tradition has often held to this precious doctrine:

> As we see from the Westminster Confession and the 1689 Baptist Confession the Puritans believed in the doctrines of grace such as election and particular redemption (Rom 8:28-30). They followed Calvin in resisting

false human rationalisations. For instance they resisted the idea that God only loves the elect and hates the non-elect. This error is called hyper-Calvinism. It is a very serious error which is recurring today. The Puritans were experts in their understanding of the concept of common grace although they did not use that term. Their teaching accords fully with the way in which the doctrine of Common Grace is expounded by Prof John Murray (cf Works). They believed that the Holy Spirit is constantly active in restraining evil and promoting good throughout society. The Puritans believed in the universal love of God for all mankind (1 Tim 2:1-6; 2 Peter 3:9). They believed in the universal provision of God for all mankind according to the covenant made with Noah as representative of the whole world (Gen 8:20-22 and Ps 145).

Many other quotes could be provided, but the point has been made: this doctrine of the sincere desire of God to bless the whole world through Jesus Christ is well represented within the Reformed tradition of theology. It was part and parcel of those Reformation doctrines that awakened Europe to the gospel, and was held by many who framed our Reformation documents and confessions. And it was explained and preached by those of the Puritan era even up to this present day. We are in good company if we cling to this truth!

# 3

This gracious invitation reveals God's heart for His creation; He loves the world and desires its salvation.

The sincerity of the gospel offer springs from God's nature of love and His desire to bless all of His creatures. As Augustine of Hippo so aptly puts it, "The cross was a pulpit in which Christ preached His love to the world" (Watson 166).

God entreats in the Old Testament: "Ho, every one that thirsteth, come ye to the waters" (Isa. 55:1). In the gospels, Jesus stood and cried, "If any man thirst, let him come unto me, and drink" (John 7:37). He also beckoned, "Come unto me, all *ye* that labour and are heavy laden, and I will give you rest" (Matt 11:28). He announced furthermore, "I am the living bread which came down from heaven: if any man eat of this bread, he shall live for ever..." (John 6:51). The final words of Scripture plead with us: "Let him that is athirst come; and whosoever will let him take the water of life freely" (Rev. 22:17). How can we deny that God truly loves mankind and desires his salvation?

Again, this inviting manner is how God has revealed Himself in Scripture. We would think it dishonest if any human offered such kind entreaties, and yet only hated those he beckoned in such loving tones. To have sweet words but a bitter disposition is the height of deception. Judas betrayed Jesus with a kiss, and those who deny the sincerity of the gospel offer paint God's action in like manner.

Those who deny God's general disposition to bless His whole creation slander Him and make Him into a pretender. They paint Him as one who convinces us of His charade and soothes us with many persuasions that are but hollow and insincere.

## BUT WHAT ABOUT JACOB AND ESAU?

In an effort to go against the *zeitgeist*, or general beliefs, of modern evangelicalism, which says that God loves each one of us exactly the same, many Calvinists assert that God loves those He chooses to love and hates those He chooses to hate, usually after quoting Romans 9:13: "Jacob have I loved, but Esau have I hated". They look no deeper into where the Bible speaks of God's love toward His creation, opting instead for an un-nuanced view that does not adequately explain His love and desire of salvation for all. The truth is not merely that God loves some and hates others, but that He also loves those He hates.

Many of the Reformers and Puritans spoke of a *"Three-Fold Love of God"* for His creatures (the love of benevolence, the love of beneficence, and the love of complacency), and that He affirmed His love in at least one of these three ways.

R.C Sproul explains the first type of love in his article "Abundant Love": "This love of benevolence, or good will, extends to all people without distinction. God is loving, in this sense, even to the damned" (par. 8).

The second type is the love of beneficence, which results in loving actions toward all. Sproul writes, "…the difference between benevolence and beneficence is the difference between disposition and action" (par. 9). Benevolence speaks of God's good intentions toward all, and beneficence speaks of the proof, or action, that is a result of those intentions. This love of beneficence is what we would call God's "common grace", for the Lord is merciful to all and shows each of His creatures some measure of kindness in this life.

The third type is God's love of complacency. Sproul writes that this kind is neither universal nor unconditional. He then explains the following: "God's love of complacency is the special delight and pleasure He takes first of all in His only-begotten Son…By adoption in Christ, every believer shares in this divine love of complacency. It is the love enjoyed by Jacob, but not by Esau. This love is reserved for the redeemed in whom God delights…" (pars. 15, 16).

If you were to ask whether God loves the Elect and hates the reprobate, or whether God loves everyone, the answer is not a simple *Yes* or *No*. The reply to both questions is actually *Yes* and *Yes*!

God loves all with some love. And in His electing decree, God loves some with all love.

We see this same thing in human affairs. I love mankind generally, but I love my wife with a special love. Thomas Aquinas in his *Summa Theologica* echoes this truth. After first asserting God's general love for every created thing, Aquinas quotes Augustine regarding the different kinds of God's love: "God loves all things that He has made, and amongst them rational creatures more, and of these especially those who are members of His only-begotten Son Himself" (115). The majority of Protestant Reformers has never veered from this long-held tenet of the ancient Church and it, too, has recognized types of God's love to all, even while affirming that God is said to hate some in His wrath.

# GOD LOVED THE RICH YOUNG RULER

One example in Scripture that illustrates this general benevolence toward all mankind is the case of the rich young ruler, that man who encountered Jesus and appeared as if he would soon believe, and yet went away sad because he would not part with his riches.

In the past, I believed this young man MUST have been saved later and not ultimately lost. His story seems to have a sad ending, but because the text states, "Then Jesus beholding him loved him" (Mark 10:21), I assumed he must have eventually come to faith. After all, I was sure Jesus loves only the elect and hates all the non-elect! My theological grid demanded I hold to assumptions not found in the text.

In my studies, I read again the parable of the Wedding Feast in Matthew 22. I marveled that the evicted guest who lacked the proper garment was still called a "friend" and not an enemy by our kind King. It began to seem as if God is tenderhearted even toward those who reject Him.

I was astounded further by the kindness of our Lord even when He was betrayed. When Judas approached Him in the Garden of Gethsemane, Jesus sincerely replied to this traitor, "Friend, wherefore art thou come?" (Matt. 26:50) *Friend.* He called Judas His friend without any hint of sarcasm or irony.

Jesus preached, "Ye have heard that it hath been said, Thou shalt love thy neighbor, and hate thine enemy" (Matt. 5:43). But He goes on to give the command, "Love your enemies" (5:44). This is precisely what God does all the time. He causes the sun to rise on the evil and the good, sends rain to the righteous and the unrighteous, and loves His enemies just as He commanded us to do.

Jesus further taught us, "For if ye love them which love you, what reward have ye? do not even the publicans the same?" (Matt. 5:46) God shows kindness and mercy to all. He does not give us an ethical standard that is not rooted in His own Being. We mirror the heart of God in our love toward all.

The theologian Arthur Pink and others have written against this belief, I know. For example, in his article "Objections to God's Sovereignty Answered", Pink says, "To tell the Christ-rejector that God loves him is to cauterize his conscience as well as to afford him a sense of security in his sins". But is the love of God no better than the love of the tax collector? Does God only love those who love Him? While I admire A.W.

Pink's writings, I believe that he was so committed to a "system of Calvinism" that to acknowledge any nuances in God's love or to posit any kind of love toward all would be to give a foothold to Arminianism.

# GOD GAINS JUDICIAL SATISFACTION FROM EXECUTING HIS WRATH, YET HE DELIGHTS IN MERCY

God loves justice. So when the fallen universe rebels against Him and He executes His wrath upon it, there is satisfaction. There are some shocking verses that speak of the righteous rejoicing over the destruction of the wicked: "Rejoice over her, *thou* heaven, and ye holy apostles and prophets; for God hath avenged you on her" (Revelation 18:20). There are others that speak of God rejoicing over the fall of unrepentant sinners: "Because I have called, and ye refused; I have stretched out my hand, and no man regarded; But ye have set at naught all my counsel, and would none of my reproof: I also will laugh at your calamity; I will mock when your fear cometh..." (Prov. 1:24-26). Psalm 37:13 tells us that the Lord laughs at the wicked, seeing that his day of judgment comes. There is joy in seeing justice done.

The same God who speaks of hating Esau, however, has also spoken with emphatic tones, even swearing by Himself that, "*As* I live, saith the Lord GOD, I have no pleasure in the death of the wicked; but that the wicked turn from his way and live: turn ye, turn ye from your evil ways; for why will ye die, O house of Israel?" (Ezek.

33:11) God does not desire the wicked to perish, but wishes they would be saved. He speaks of mercy as being His delight: "Who *is* a God like unto thee, that pardoneth iniquity, and passeth by the transgression of the remnant of his heritage? He retaineth not his anger for ever, because he delighteth in mercy" (Micah 7:18).

God is said to hate, yet never is it said that, *"God is hate"*. On the contrary, not only does He extend love to all His creatures in some form or fashion, but He is also said to be love (1 John 4:8). Though He punishes sin, hates the wicked, and executes judgment, His nature is love, and He extends this love to all of His creatures: "For it is God's nature to be kind, and to give happiness" (Henry, *Concise Bible Commentary*, 1 John 4:7).

Thus it is not proper to simply say that God hates some and loves others without qualification, as if He is equally inclined toward both dispositions. No, God's nature is beneficent and His disposition is to bless all.

Does this mean that God loves everybody in a generic sense? Well, yes and no. If you mean that God loves each person in the way most people mean it, as in a love that is exactly the same and absent of judicial hatred for the wicked, then no. But if you mean that God has regard and beneficence toward all His creatures, shows them kindness, exercises a delay in their punishment, gives them many mercies in this life, and is disposed to bless them, then yes, God's love extends to all.

Reformed author Michael Horton sums up this distinction in God's love: "God loves the world and calls everyone in the world to Christ *outwardly* through the Gospel, and yet God loves the elect with a saving purpose and calls them by His Spirit *inwardly* through the same Gospel (John 6:63–64; 10:3–5, 11, 14–18, 25–30; Acts 13:48; Rom. 8:28–30; 2 Tim. 1:9)".

# THE JUDGE AND THE SNIPER

Now you may ask, do sinners make God eternally unhappy? If a man hates God, refuses to turn, and ends up in hell, does he gain some sort of victory (though costly) to frustrate God?

No, he does not. God gains satisfaction in all of His works. The sinner in hell will not be gratified in knowing he has made God sad or has thwarted God's divine plan.

Many become confused at this point and I understand why. First, God delights in His glory. Second, He is glorified when His wrath is poured out on sinners; His justice is magnified. Third, God does not delight in the death of the wicked but desires them to turn from their sins (Ezek. 18:23). But how does this add up? Let me try to explain.

We get a penal satisfaction when we see justice done even though we may grieve the offense. For example, I will never charge WWII soldiers with sin when they cheered at the news of Hitler's death. They had every reason to celebrate. Yet the death of any man is a loss. When I heard we finally killed Osama Bin Laden, I rejoiced. I don't believe this was sin. In fact, I was sobered by the knowledge that a never-dying soul went to its reward. Yet I believe there are rightful emotions

34

felt on such an occasion—joy over seeing justice done, relief over seeing a threat eliminated, satisfaction over seeing an ordeal or trial finished—even as we are sobered by what it cost to vindicate justice and what it took to make things right. When any man dies, it is a sobering thing. There is a certain sadness to it. Yet at the same time, when evil tyrants die, it is no sin to celebrate such occasions.

As an example of this conundrum—wrestling with sadness and joy over justice—imagine a judge. A heinous murderer enters his courtroom. Remorseless, the prisoner stands before him for sentencing. All the evidence seals his guilt. There are plenty of witnesses. He is an evil man. Though in our day this is not popular, a just judge would hand down the death penalty to this murderer, and he would be executed without excessive delay. Now imagine if this criminal was immediately hung in front of the victims and the community.

What are the rightful emotions for this judge? When he goes home to his wife and she asks him, *"Did you have a good day at work? Do you enjoy your job? Do you take pleasure in what you do?"* how might he respond? Although he might feel satisfaction that he administered justice to a wicked criminal, he must also live with the knowledge that a man died because of his decision. He delivered justice by decreeing death. And that is a serious and heavy responsibility.

Here is a second example. I read a swat team sniper's account in which an armed criminal robbed a bank and took hostages. This sniper was called to the scene where he watched as the gunman broadcasted his intentions to shoot the hostages, killing one every 20 minutes. As he brought the first captive out, however, the gunman made a mistake. He allowed two feet of distance between himself and his prisoner. The sniper saw his opportunity then and there and shot the criminal directly in the head. The man lurched backwards, dead, and the swat team charged forward and freed the hostages.

What are the rightful emotions for this sniper? Though he felt satisfaction over a job well done, he also experienced sadness over the loss of life. It is a shame it had to come to this, and yet he was praised and rewarded. He wrote that he felt fortunate to be there and glad to help put right a situation that was going wrong in order to protect the innocent.

I believe the judge and the sniper could say that they both love and hate their jobs. As the judge hands out the death sentence to the murderer, he does a praiseworthy thing—a thing in which he can take pride. And yet he may not desire to do it at all; he merely does as justice demands. Even as he gains satisfaction in it, he simultaneously regrets it. Likewise, as the sniper squeezes the trigger, he feels both the regret of taking a life and the relief that the threat is eliminated. His skill is proved true and the evil is contained. Yet both the judge and the sniper wish things had not come to this, call the results regrettable, and state a desire that all could have lived happily and without evil.

We can also look at it another way. When a child disobeys, does his parent want to spank him? Does his parent want to see him punished? No. Usually, parents do not desire to discipline their children even though they are willing to. It is a regretful but necessary thing due to the child's wrongdoing. They take no pleasure in the punishment even as they proceed with it.

In the same way, God does not gleefully cast men into hell. He possesses holy wrath and hates sinners (this is shocking to many modern Christians), but His normal mode of government is one of blessing. His nature is that of love. He sends people to hell only after many mercies and, for many, after countless kind entreaties through the gospel. He gains glory from the execution of His wrath and all of heaven will echo "amen" at His righteous judgments. Yet those judgments are only executed after He in His kindness has patiently endured the wicked for many long years. Romans 9:22 says, "*What* if God, willing to shew *his* wrath, and to make his power known, endured with much longsuffering the vessels of wrath fitted to destruction..."

Because of our sin, none of us deserves to be a recipient of God's love. But He nonetheless loves us according to His divine choice. While we acknowledge that He hates sinners, He exercises a creaturely love toward all, takes no pleasure in their deaths, and even entreats them repeatedly with the gospel.

While the above doctrine is not as tidy as the simple doctrine that, *"God loves some and hates others to His glory,"* or that *"God loves everybody exactly the same and wills all to be saved,"* we are nonetheless stuck with it, for that is what the Bible teaches. Did we expect the God of the universe NOT to strain our understanding? Scripture often gives a more complex approach than can easily fit within our categories of systematic theology. None of this is contrary to reason or illogical, yet it often stretches our reason to meditate on these matters. Even we fallible creatures can relate to how we can possess both love and judgment concerning some soul. How much greater is God's capacity for such things?

Though older theologians may not label it as such, this general love for all mankind has come to be known as God's common grace. Some deny altogether that this common grace exists, or they assert that it is actually not grace at all, for the end result—the rejection of all of these divine kindnesses—is only further judgment for sin.

But the reality is that God has not set a trap for man. His actions stem from love, not from a desire to "fatten up" the reprobate for the day of slaughter. Though greater condemnation is reaped through the repeated rejections of God's invitations, His acts of love are no strategy to give the wicked more kindling for their day of burning. If anyone spurns such love as this, then God uses that rejection to increase the person's guilt and punishment. But He truly means good to mankind when He is good to them. He is not insincere in His acts of kindness.

Samuel Waldron, exposing the 1689 Baptist Confession of Faith, explains as follows:

> The Bible teaches that the good gifts which God bestows upon men in general, including the non-elect, are manifestations of God's general love and common grace towards

them (Matt. 5:43-48; Luke 6:35; Acts 14:17). While they do serve to increase the guilt of those who misuse them, this is not the sole intention of God towards the non-elect in giving them. The Scriptures teach that God desires the good even of those who never come to experience the good wished for them by God (Deut. 5:29; 32:29; Ps. 81:13-16; Isa. 48:18). The Scriptures also teach that God so loved sinners that in the person of his Son he weeps because of the destruction they bring upon themselves (Matt. 23:37; Luke 13:34; 19:41-44). God emphatically expresses his desire that some should repent who do not repent (Ezek. 18:23, 32; 33:11; Rom. 10:11). The Scriptures teach a general gospel call which comes to the hearers of the gospel indiscriminately and which may be, and often is resisted (Prov. 1:24; 8:4; Isa. 50:2; 65:12; 66:4; Jer. 7:13-14; 35:17; Matt. 22:14). (121-122)

Even as God hates sinners, He blesses them in many ways. He loves them as His creatures even though He has not elected their full number. He chooses not to execute in His decretive will—His sovereign plan we will never fully understand—everything He is said to desire in His prescriptive will—His revealed desires as found in Scripture.

In other words, for God to more greatly reveal Himself and more fully manifest His character for His greater glory, He has chosen not to ordain everything He desires.

(See APPENDIX A for a fuller treatment of this theme.)

# THE BATTLE OVER JOHN 3:16

John 3:16 has often proven to be ground zero in debates over God's predestination versus man's responsibility. Many Calvinists seek to deny this piece of ground to the enemy and so interpret John 3:16 through a "Calvinistic lens" lest they grant any room to the Arminian.

But listen well:

*There are no Calvinist verses or Arminian verses—only Bible verses.*

We need not fear if an offer of salvation appears to be universal in Scripture, nor should we push for partisan interpretations of the text. The Bible should determine our systematic theology, not vice versa.

In many reformed sermons on John 3:16, preachers frequently spend so much time explaining who God DOESN'T love that they seem to forget the main focus of the text is the magnitude and hugeness of God's love and His manner of showing that love. As one minister put it well, "They seem to be more concerned about shutting the gate to the reprobate than opening it for the elect!"

In contrast, remember the already-quoted John Calvin and Matthew Henry in their respective commentaries on John 3:16: "...the Heavenly Father loves the human race, and wishes that they should not perish" (Calvin). And, "Though many of the world of mankind perish, yet God's giving his only-begotten Son was an instance of his love to the whole world, because through him there is a general offer of life and salvation made to all" (Henry 1540).

The focus of John 3:16 is not on the extent of the word "world". Rather, it centers upon the greatness and quality of God's love. It deals not so much with the recipients of God's love as it does with the Benefactor—our kind, merciful God.

Now, if you corner me on what "world" means here, my answer is this: humankind. Man is in view here—i.e., not merely the elect world, but the entirety of lost humanity. After all, this passage goes on to speak of the "world" as rejecting God and perishing just three verses later: "light is come into the world, and men loved darkness rather than light, because their deeds were evil" (John 3:19). How can it be that "world" can mean the world of the elect in verse 16, and then in the very same breath mean the reprobate a few verses later? It simply does not. Verse 17 informs us, "For God sent not his Son into the world to condemn the world; but that the world through him might be saved" (John 3:17). But why would God send His Son into the world to condemn the elect (if indeed "world" here means the world of the elect)? This verse makes perfect sense, however, if the world that is spoken of refers to humanity generally.

We need not limit the scope of "world" in this text at all because the passage itself limits it with the provision of "whosoever". Who has Christ died for? Whosoever believeth! That is the limitation.

D.A. Carson echoes this view when he writes the following:

> I know that some try to take kosmos
> ("world") here to refer to the elect. But that
> really will not do. All the evidence of the
> usage of the word in John's gospel is against
> the suggestion. True, *world* in John does
> not so much refer to bigness as to badness.
> In John's vocabulary, *world* is primarily the
> moral order in willful and culpable rebellion
> against God. In John 3:16 God's love in
> sending the Lord Jesus is to be admired not
> because it is extended to so big a thing as
> the world, but to so bad a thing; not to so
> many people, as to such a wicked people...
> On the axis, God's love for the world cannot
> be collapsed into his love for the elect. (17)

J.C. Ryle, respected by even the strictest of Calvinists, agrees:

> For one thing, it seems to me a violent
> straining of language to confine the
> word "world" to the elect. "The world" is

undoubtedly a name sometimes given to the
"wicked" exclusively. But I cannot see it is
a name ever given to the saints...The true
view of the words "God so loved the world",
I believe to be this. The "world" means the
whole human race of mankind, both saints
and sinners, without any exception. (156-
157)

Much fault is to be found in many Reformed
sermons on John 3:16. If your form of Calvinism causes
you to preach this text in such a way that the question
of who God doesn't love is the focus rather than the
full and astounding intensity of His love, then you
poorly represent the reason John wrote this verse. The
emphasis is on God's love—not on God's non-love—
toward His creation. John 3:16 is Good News—an
invitation of mercy showing the beneficence of God to
sinful mankind.

# 4

This kind disposition of God to bless His creatures fuels our desire to see the whole world blessed. We mirror the heart of God when we desire the salvation of the lost.

God's love is shown in His many kind and ardent entreaties! Deuteronomy 5:29 says, "O that there were such an heart in them, that they would fear me, and keep all my commandments..." Psalm 81:13 states, "Oh that my people had hearkened unto me, *and* Israel had walked in my ways!" And Ezekiel 18:31 asks, "... why will ye die, O house of Israel?" These verses throb with urgency for the souls of men to turn to God.

How can we do anything other than plead with sinners in the same manner as God? He is our Divine Model! In fact, in our pleadings it is God Himself beseeching men through us to be reconciled to Him: "Now then we are ambassadors for Christ, as though God did beseech *you* by us: we pray *you* in Christ's stead, be ye reconciled to God" (2 Cor. 5:20).

And if we are to strive to be godly (i.e., like God) in our actions and sentiments, does this mean that I have more compassion than God Himself when I offer the gospel to the lost indiscriminately? That my compassion stretches beyond the supposed confines of God's love? That my sincerity for the lost exceeds God's sincerity? That when I invite people to repent with an earnest desire for their salvation, I am inviting them with a sincerity that is absent in God?

No! Not at all. We mirror the heart of God when we desire the good of all people, especially their eternal good.

Harold Dekker, who served as a professor of missions at Calvin Theological Seminary, states that our sentiments and actions ought to mirror God's dispositions and actions toward the lost:

> When Jesus taught His followers to love their enemies, the clear premise of His precept was the fact that God loves His enemies (Matt. 5:43-45 and Luke 6:35). Already in Proverbs came the lofty injunction: "If thine enemy be hungry, give him bread to eat; and if he be thirsty, give him water to drink" (Prov. 25:21). Is then the servant greater than his Lord? Is the creature nobler than the Creator? God loves His enemies; God loves all men.

We see this heart of God in the tears of Paul in Romans 9: "I say the truth in Christ, I lie not, my conscience also bearing me witness in the Holy Ghost, that I have great heaviness and continual sorrow in my heart. For *I could wish that myself were accursed from Christ for my brethren*, my kinsmen according to the flesh..." (Rom. 9:1-3, emphasis added). Despite knowing that a great many of the Jews would be lost, Paul still sincerely longs for their salvation.

Let me ask you this question concerning the above passage: is Paul praiseworthy when he wishes himself accursed for the sake of his fellow Jews' salvation, or should he be rebuked for illogical sentimentalism contrary to the nature of God?

Paul's sentiments are commendable here. He can wish himself accursed for his brethren's sake because he walked the steps and shared the heart of his Lord Jesus Christ, who was condemned and stood actually accursed by God for the sake of His people.

We see this same heart of God in Robert Murray McCheyne, a missionary from the 19th Century who evangelistically preached the sincere, seeking love of God as a reason for hearers to close with—receive as Savior—the Christ offered in the gospel:

> Though you have no care for your soul, yet Christ has, and wishes to save it. Though you do not care for Christ, yet He cares for [you], and stretches out his hands to you. Christ did not come to the earth because people were caring about their souls, but because we were lost. You are only the more lost. Christ is all the more seeking you. This day you may find a Saviour, "Unto you, O men, I call." (325)

The love of God toward sinners motivates our own love toward sinners.

# AGAIN I ASK, AM I MORE COMPASSIONATE THAN GOD?

As Jesus neared Jerusalem, He wept upon seeing the city and desired the salvation of her inhabitants (Luke 19; Matthew 23). Commenting on these tears, John Calvin writes in his *Harmony of the Gospels*, "... he wished that his coming might bring salvation to all".

Yet when I have asked High Calvinists about these tears, I have had several explain them as merely due to Christ's human nature, part of His humanity only.

Should we imagine then that Jesus in human flesh is more compassionate than God? Or that these tears were a mere human defect experienced during His earthly ministry? Is not Christ the perfect image of the invisible God? And is not His human will in perfect cooperation and harmony with the Divine Will of God within Him? Is He not inseparably true God and true man?

At the sixth ecumenical council (Constantinople III, 681), the Church confessed that Christ possesses two wills and two natural operations—divine and human—which are not opposed to each other in the least, but rather cooperate fully. Christ's human will does not, therefore, oppose or contradict His divine will—His two natures being joined together in perfect harmony without confusion. And it is this God-Man who wept for lost souls, knowing full well their future. And by doing so, Christ revealed the heart of God to us.

Shouldn't we as missionaries—ambassadors for Christ—strive to model this heart of Jesus as He wept before Jerusalem? Is there some discord between God in human flesh and God Himself, and if so, which should we emulate? Or rather, is there perfect Trinitarian harmony regarding God's loving disposition to bless His creatures, and do we enter into that fellowship and gain this same heart when we are saved?

While we don't assert that the glorified Christ on His throne in heaven still cries tears, we are not to posit that His exaltation denuded His compassion from Him, nor should we insinuate that such compassion was a weakness of human nature rather than a noble and commendable display of divine love. No! He is the ever-compassionate God.

Even worse, some High Calvinists suppose that Christ's desire for the souls of those unrepentant sinners in Jerusalem was a sham. One writer asserts precisely that, "Such expressions, then, are intended to instruct the hearers as to what their passion ought to be, not to indicate that God is characterized by such passions Himself". In effect, then, God is saying, *"Do as I pretend to do....perform as I feign to do...not as I really am."* He thus becomes an insincere actor, like a movie starlet simulating love onscreen, yet dispassionate or even hateful behind the scenes. These writers suppose that Christ cried crocodile tears over Jerusalem.

I cannot imagine it controversial or provocative to assert that God actually wants sinners to be saved, or that His kindness is meant to lead them to repentance (Romans 2:4). Are His mercies but snares, as food and sweets are to rats fixed upon a trap? No! "The LORD *is* good to all: and his tender mercies *are* over all his works" (Psalm 145:9).

God's offers are evidences of His love. God loves his creatures, and so He warns them of the wrath to come. This isn't the smug declaration of an older brother holding some dainty just out of a toddler's reach and mocking, *"Oh, do you want this?"* These are kind entreaties from our beneficent Creator.

God entreats man generally to be saved without marking any distinction between elect and non-elect. The call goes out to all; the invitation is proffered with no exceptions, and therefore we conclude that the heart that offered this invitation goes out to all. God has revealed a general compassion for all of His creatures and a general desire for their well being.

This attitude is worthy of our imitation! *Oh God, please give me the same heart Jesus Christ displayed before Jerusalem. Let my heart be moved by the plight of the lost, and let me have compassion for those who need Thee, in Jesus' name, Amen!*

Some High Calvinists may further object that I am focusing too much on God's revealed will when, in fact, God's secret will is much different. My answer is simply, again, that this language of God's love and desire toward all is the language the Holy Spirit sees fit to use. The God who inspired the entire Scriptures also inspired these very particular words such that, though we cannot know God comprehensively, we can learn of Him through the manner He has chosen to reveal Himself. And this manner is as a loving God who desires the salvation of mankind. The Scriptures utilize the language of "wish", "desire", and "pleasure" to describe God's revealed will concerning the salvation of all men. I must represent God as He has chosen to represent Himself.

Some High Calvinists still persist and remind us that any such emotional language of God is merely anthropopathism—ascribing human emotions to a deity. Yet 1 John 4:8 is clearly not such a phrase, but expresses an ontological statement about God, namely, that God is love. This speaks of God's very Being Himself. Though human language about God may be analogical, this does not mean it is not true. God Himself has chosen to reveal His nature through the words of Scripture, and we must take His Word to be reliable and informative. The Bible abounds in statements about God's lovingkindness toward His creation and about His loving Being. Such statements cannot merely be brushed off as figurative.

## A NOTE ON CURRENT EVENTS AMONG REFORMED BAPTISTS

In recent years, Reformed Baptists have taken a renewed interest in how God interacts with His creation. Discussion and debate have come to focus on the narrow topic of divine impassibility, the doctrine that God cannot suffer nor does He have passions like unto men. There have been variations in how different pastors have each expressed this truth that God is without *"body, parts, or passions"*. I won't be stepping into this impassibility debate here, but want to warn the reader that many Reformed Baptists have rejected this doctrine of the sincere free offer of the gospel due to the false conclusion that one's view of strict impassibility requires a denial of God's sincerity in the gospel call. No such conclusion is warranted, however.

Many Reformed theologians count a rejection of this doctrine of God's sincere and well-meant offer of the gospel to be one of the chief tenets of Hyper-Calvinism. Any shift away from this doctrine is a shift toward Hyperism and toward a heritage like that of the Gospel Standard Baptists and the Hardshell Baptists rather than the grand heritage of William Carey, Andrew Fuller, and all those who did so much for world missions. Whatever one's views on impassibility, there is no way that Reformed Baptists may deny the sincere free offer and remain a healthy body (as seen in the next section).

# 5

---

If we do not believe these truths,
our passion for missions may suffer and we may
grow cold toward the lost.

---

Why should we plead with sinners and desire their salvation? Because God pleads with sinners and desires their salvation.

But what if God does not actually desire their salvation? Should we?

This doctrine of the sincere free offer of the gospel is most vital for us to retain, for with this doctrine stands or falls our hearts' warmth in evangelism and our zeal for souls.

If you believe that God has mere simple hatred and no accompanying love for vast numbers of our fellow creatures, then you may have no love for the lost. If you believe that God is void of any true, sincere desire for blessings on all of His creation, then you may have coldness in your soul toward others. If you believe that God does not invite all by the gospel, then you may not invite all.

The great Baptist preacher Charles Spurgeon knew this and he writes, "Some of my Brethren are greatly scandalized by the general invitations which I am in the habit of giving to sinners, as sinners. Some of them go the length of asserting that there are no universal invitations in the Word of God."

In fact, the modern missionary movement emerged among the Calvinistic English Baptists in a milieu of opposition and writing against High Calvinism. Carey's friend and advocate Andrew Fuller wrote the devastating *The Gospel Worthy of All Acceptation* in opposition to those who denied the appropriateness of inviting sinners indiscriminately to believe. As a consequence of these doctrines, churches shrank and shrank, causing Fuller to write, "Had matters gone on but a few years longer, the Baptists would have become a perfect dunghill in society."

If you believe that God's decree to reprobate (and thus hate) the non-elect occurs prior to His will to permit the Fall of mankind such that His decree of reprobation is divorced from prior human sinfulness, then you could tend toward indifference regarding the eternal fate of others.

Some High Calvinists deny the gospel to be an offer and assert that it is a mere command or statement of fact. Yet those who abide by either the Westminster Confession of Faith or the 2nd London Baptist Confession of Faith (the 1689 Baptist Confession) must believe the gospel to be an offer and not merely a command, for that is how the London confession describes it in chapter 7: "...it pleased the *Lord* to make a *Covenant* of *Grace* wherein he freely offereth unto *Sinners,* Life and Salvation by *Jesus Christ*...". He "freely offereth".

God's very nature is "plenteous in mercy". Psalm 86 says, "For thou, Lord, art good, and *ready to forgive*; and *plenteous in mercy* unto all them that call upon thee" (Ps. 86:5, emphasis added). Isaiah echoes the abundant love of our Lord in chapter 55: "Let the wicked forsake his way, and the unrighteous man his thoughts: and let him return unto the LORD, and he will have mercy upon him; and to our God, for he will *abundantly pardon*" (Isa. 55:7). Abundance in pardon, plenteous mercy, and a readiness to forgive are not words of a stiff offer or a begrudged serving of salvation. Rather, they are words that speak of God's *desire* for our salvation unto His glory. He is "ready to forgive". Case closed.

If you believe that the kind invitation of the gospel is merely a statement of fact rather than God actually beseeching souls to be reconciled to Him, then your heart will likely never warm to the spiritual needs of the world, and you may never beseech and plead with souls to be reconciled to God.

If you believe that the offer of the gospel is a mere indifferent one and not a sincere or well-meant one, and that God has not put His heart into it, then you may acquire a smug and glib view of the fate of souls. *"Here is the truth, take it or leave it…it is of no difference to me either way!"*

## DUTY VERSUS DESIRE

Suppose I buy my wife roses every first of the month out of sheer duty but no true desire. Would such an attitude joined to my action kindle the flames of romance? Or would it deaden them?

In like manner, suppose God's preachers merely performed their duty of evangelism in offering the gospel without any sincerity behind it. Would this increase or decrease evangelistic zeal?

Contrast this cold temperament with the urgency and sincerity of that wonderful preacher Joseph Alleine, who implores, "The God that made you most graciously invites you. His most sweet and merciful nature invites you. O the kindness of God, His boundless compassion, His tender mercies!"

Even more ridiculous would be to protest thusly, *"I do indeed possess a white-hot sincerity in my evangelistic efforts to see all the lost saved! But I deny that God has this same sincerity toward the lost."* Thus we posit as admirable an incongruity between our will and the will of our Creator.

If we defend our own desire for all to be saved and yet deny it in our God, we make all prayers ridiculous when we pray, *"Let me be conformed to Your will, oh Lord!"*

Or we charge the Apostle Paul with sinful ignorance in Romans 9 for wishing himself accursed for the sake of his Jewish countrymen. Again, I ask: was this expression of Paul ("I could wish that myself were accursed from Christ for my brethren, my kinsmen according to the flesh" [Rom. 9:3]) a commendable sentiment and worthy to be emulated? Or must we excuse it as a foolish outburst of emotion?

Suppose, as well, that you are married and that your wife acquiesces to your intimate desires for lovemaking out of mere duty's sake, but not due to pleasure or sincere desire of her own. Would this increase or decrease your closeness, ardor, and affection?

In like manner, it is astounding to believe that God would offer the gospel to the world without any sincere desire for it to be saved. To believe that the gospel is a cold command and not an earnest invitation, and that this cold command in God is to be met by our own white-hot zeal is incoherent. This is but poor fuel to nourish evangelistic warmth. Can an ice cube be used to spark a flame?

I can draw no other conclusion from the Scriptures than this: eternal life through Jesus Christ is freely offered to all sinners, and God's invitations are sincere and well meant.

In the preaching of the gospel to all, the love of God is set before all men, and the human race is indiscriminately invited. All who are thirsty may come and drink, and all who are weary may come and rest. God's essential disposition toward all of His creatures is a disposition to bless. He delights to save. The gospel offer is free. If you desire to come to Jesus, He will not turn you away, but rather will delight in your salvation.

As a missionary, I desire to display this same kind disposition to all. I desire to mirror the heart of God in my actions.

# CONCLUSION

"*D*o you believe that God really wants to save even *me?*" The man standing before me repeated his query urgently yet tentatively.

"*Yes, absolutely,*" I replied without hesitation. "*In fact, He would rejoice to do so even now. It would be as if He were to run to greet you before you even arrived. As if He were to hike up his robes as the father of the prodigal son did and run to his child, forsaking all dignified bearing in order to embrace one who had come afresh from the pigsty. Heaven would rejoice at your salvation.*"

I could almost see the burden physically melt from his shoulders. The tension, the nervousness, the weight of his sins, the doubt that God could love *even him*, dissipated with my words of hope—with God's promise and offer of an eternity with Him. All he had to do was repent and believe. That man was rightly comforted.

Properly understood, the gospel is truly good news! It is not a mere judicial decree handed down by a distant judge, but the warm appeal of a loving Savior.

*Lord, make our hearts and our affections the same as Thine, amen!*

In fact, found in the writings of the Puritan Samuel Rutherford is just such a case as mine—the case of a doubting man who wonders whether or not God really wants him to be saved. See how Rutherford answers below. Note well that Rutherford was one of the Scottish Commissioners to the Westminster Assembly, and you will better understand what he means in chapter 7 when he asserts that the Lord "freely offereth unto sinners life and salvation by Jesus Christ...":

> But if the sinner be wearied and laden, and sees, though through a cloud only, Christ only must help and save; if not, he is utterly and eternally lost. What is there upon Christ's part to hinder thee to believe, O guilty wretch? Oh, (saith he,) I fear Christ only offers Himself to me, but he minds no salvation to me? Answer: Is not this to raise an evil report and slander on the Holy One of Israel? For Christ's offer is really an offer, and in so far, it is real love, though it cannot infer the love of election to glory, yet the total denial of this offer opens up the black seal of reprobation to heathens without the church. And therefore it is love to thee, if thou be humbled for sin; 2. And have half an eye to the unsearchable riches of gospel mercy; 3. And be self-condemned; 4. And have half a desire of Christ: thou mayest expound love by love, and lay hold on the promise, and be saved. An error of humble love to Christ, is no error. (302-303)

I am glad to know that the answer to my own doubting man's query mirrors Rutherford's.

# A SINCERE INVITATION

Dear Reader,

Perhaps as you have read this treatment of the gospel, you have wondered if it is truly for you. Perhaps you have grown up in the church but have never experienced a genuine relationship with Christ the Savior of the world. Perhaps you feel something is missing from your life.

If this is you, I would like to appeal to you: by the grace of our loving Savior, *anyone* can take the free and sincere offer of the gospel. *Anyone* can be overwhelmed by the love and kindness of God and embrace Jesus Christ. We have *all* rejected His kind mercies from birth. But it is not too late. He has provided a way for us to turn from our abject rejection and depravity and come to Him for life, rest, fulfillment, and grace. If the Lord of the universe, Jesus Christ Himself, wept over them that would not be saved, how gladly would He receive even you, even now, if you are willing to embrace His tender invitations?

Dear Reader…how He would delight to save you— He came to seek and to save the lost (Luke 19:10)! How quickly He would embrace you. Would you embrace Him even today?

In the words of Richard Alleine, that great evangelistic preacher of the Puritan era, we see how the sincere love of God and desire for the salvation of all spills over into the pleas of His servants:

> I tell you again, I wish you well; and not only I, but the Lord God that hath sent me to you: The Lord Jesus wishes you well; he wishes and wooes, wooes and weeps, weeps and dies, that your Souls might live, and be blessed for ever: He hath once more sent me to you, even to the worst amongst you, to tell you from him, that he's unwilling you should perish; that he hath a kindness for you in his heart, if you will accept it: He hath Blood and Bowels for you; Blood to expiate your guilt, to wash away your filth; and Bowels to offer you the benefit of his Blood; with this Wish, Oh that it were theirs! Oh that they would hearken and accept!

I wish you all the best in life—and that which is best is Jesus Christ.

All is confirmed by an open and general invitation to mankind, to come and partake freely of the promises and of the privileges of the gospel. The Spirit, by the sacred word, and by convictions and influence in the sinner's conscience, says, Come to Christ for salvation; and the bride, or the whole church, on earth and in heaven, says, Come and share our happiness. Lest any should hesitate, it is added, Let whosoever will, or, is willing, come and take of the water of life freely. May every one who hears or reads these words, desire at once to accept the gracious invitation.

—Henry, Rev. 22:17,
*Concise Bible Commentary*

# APPENDIX A

## GOD IS SAID TO DESIRE SOME THINGS WHICH HE HAS CHOSEN NOT TO ENACT

One objection that has been laid against this precious doctrine of the sincere and well-meant offer of the gospel is the following one: *"But if God wants to do something, He will do it. How is it possible that God would desire something (i.e., salvation for all) and it not come to pass?"* He is God, after all.

And I can only answer that as strange as it sounds, God is said to desire some things in Scripture that He has seen fit not to ordain. God's will is one, and yet that will has two aspects, His prescriptive or revealed will (those stated desires whereby He tells us what He wants or what is pleasing to Him) and His decretive or secret will (those things which He has ordained should come to pass). Some have referred to these two aspects of God's will as God's "will of command" and His "will of decree". Historically, Reformed scholars have seen two aspects of God's will, the *voluntas signi* (His will of sign or His revealed will), and the *voluntas beneplaciti* (will of good pleasure/decretive will). God's decretive will— what He has sovereignly ordained shall come to pass— can never be resisted, and yet His revealed will—what

He desires and has commanded us in His Word—is resisted every day.

God's revealed and secret will are not always the same. Deuteronomy 5:29, for instance, shows that all God commands in His prescriptive (revealed) will does not occur in His decretive (secret) will: "O that there were such an heart in them, that they would fear me, and keep all my commandments always, that it might be well with them, and with their children for ever!" A desire is expressed in this statement, but this desire is not met by the children of Israel, for they did not keep the commandments of God. Was this in accordance with God's will or not? No, according to His prescriptive (revealed/desired) will. But yes, according to His decretive (secret/sovereignly ordained) will.

Take this passage in 1 Thessalonians as well, which tells us, "For this is the will of God, *even* your sanctification, that ye should abstain from fornication" (1 Thess. 4:3). Yet King David and other believers have fallen into sexual sin. How is it then the will of God? It is His stated prescriptive will.

Jonathan Edwards lists other examples in Volume II of his collected works: "We and they know it was God's secret will, that Abraham should not sacrifice his son Isaac; but yet his command was, that he should do it. We know that God willed, that Pharaoh's heart should be hardened; and yet that the hardness of his heart was sin."

The Puritan William Perkins gives two examples in his work, *A Treatise of God's Free Grace, and Man's Free Will*—the example of Christ's desire to see those in Jerusalem saved, and the example of a judge condemning a guilty man—examples I used in the main text of this article.

First, the example of Jerusalem:

> There is but one will in God: yet doth it not equally will all things, but in divers respects it doth will and nill the same thing. He wills the conversion of Jerusalem, in that he approves it as a good thing in itself: in that he commands it, and exhorts men to it: in that he gives them all outward means of their conversion. He wills it not, in that he did not decree effectually to work their conversion. For God doth approve, and he may require many things, which nevertheless for just causes known to himself, he will not do. (Perkins)

Second, the example of a judge: "A judge in compassion approves and will[s] the life of a malefactour: and yet withall he wills the execution of justice in his death. Even so God sometimes wills that in his signifying will, which he wills not in the will of his good pleasure" (Perkins).

Concerning the salvation of the lost, God states a desire that they be saved. He desires that they turn and not die. Yes, He desires the salvation of all men and takes no pleasure in the death of the wicked.

And yet God has a greater desire—His own glory. For His glory and for the greater display of that glory in its fullness, to include the whole of His Divine Being (both His mercy and His justice, both His grace and His wrath, both His love and His holiness), God ordains to pass by some sinners, leaving them in their sin and guilt and allowing them to perish.

And so God is said to desire some things that do not come to pass because He has chosen, for greater reasons (such as the exalting and displaying of His full character in all its completeness), to allow them to transgress His stated desires.

Calvin tackles this issue in the following quote from his commentary on II Peter:

> So wonderful is his love towards mankind, that he would have them all to be saved, and is of his own self prepared to bestow salvation on the lost... But it may be asked, If God wishes none to perish, why is it that so many do perish? To this my answer is, that no mention is here made of the hidden purpose of God, according to which the reprobate are doomed to their own ruin, but only of his will as made known to us in the gospel. For God there stretches forth his hand without a difference to all, but lays hold only of those, to lead them to himself, whom he has chosen before the foundation of the world.

Louis Berkhof also writes:

> We believe that God "unfeignedly," that is,
> sincerely or in good faith, calls all those
> who are living under the gospel to believe,
> and offers them salvation in the way of faith
> and repentance...The offer of salvation
> in the way of faith and repentance does
> not pretend to be a revelation of the secret
> counsel of God, more specifically, of His
> design in giving Christ as an atonement for
> sin. It is simply the promise of salvation of
> all those who accept Christ by faith. This
> offer, in so far as it is universal, is always
> conditioned by faith and conversion.
> Moreover it is contingent on a faith and
> repentance such as can only be wrought in
> the heart of man by the operation of the
> Holy Spirit. The universal offer of salvation
> does not consist in the declaration that
> Christ made atonement for every man that
> hears the gospel, and that God really intends
> to save each one... It is not the duty of the
> preacher to harmonise the secret counsel of
> God respecting the redemption of sinners
> with His declarative will as expressed in the
> universal offer of salvation. He is simply an
> official ambassador, whose duty it is to carry
> out the will of the Lord in preaching the
> gospel to all men indiscriminately.... (397-
> 398)

We must affirm what the Scriptures teach even when we do not grasp it. We must not conclude that God's desire for the lost is a sham one. As Calvin writes in *Secret Providence,* "...God gives no pretended commands, but seriously declares what he wishes and approves..." God has made it plain in His Word that it is pleasing for all who hear to turn and believe. Others may contest the logic of this or rationalize away this desire, but I dare not. In the words of John Murray:

> Again, the expression "God desires," in the formula that crystallizes the crux of the question, is intended to notify not at all the "seeming" attitude of God but a real attitude, a real disposition of lovingkindness inherent in the free offer to all, in other words, a pleasure or delight in God, contemplating the blessed result to be achieved by compliance with the overture proffered and the invitation given.

Yes, God wants you to be saved. And He really means it!

# WORKS CITED

Alleine, Joseph. *An Alarm to Unconverted Sinners.* Tony Byrne, pp. 202-205. https://reformedbooksonline.com/topics/topics-by-subject/the-sincere-free-offer-of-the-gospel/joseph-alleine-on-the-sincere-free-offer-of-the-gospel/.

Alleine, Richard. *The Godly Man's Portion and Sanctuary Opened, in Two Sermons.* London, n.p., n.d., 1663, pp. 166-170. http://theologicalmeditations.blogspot.com/search/label/Richard%20Alleine.

Anonymous. "I Sought the Lord, and Afterward I Knew." *United Methodist Hymnal*, 1989, http://www.hymnary.org/text/i_sought_the_lord_and_afterward_i_knew.

Aquinas, Thomas. "Question 20, God's Love, Third Article." *Summa Theologica*, vol. 1, Part 1, Cosmo Classics, New York, 1911, pp. 113–117, https://books.google.com/books?id=gaocysd9w94c&pg=pa115&lpg=pa115&dq=.

Beeke, Joel. *A Puritan Theology.* "The Puritans on Coming to Christ." https://reformedbooksonline.com/topics/topics-by-subject/the-sincere-free-offer-of-the-gospel/the-sincere-free-offer-of-the-gospel-in-the-canons-of-dort/.

Berkhof, Louis. *Systematic Theology.* Banner of Truth Edition, VI, Grand Rapids, MI, W.B. Eerdmans Pub. Co., 1950.

*The Bible. King James Version,* Thomas Nelson Inc., 1970.

Boston, Thomas. "The Whole Works of the Late Reverend and Learned Mr. Thomas Boston." *The Whole Works of the Late Reverend and Learned Mr. Thomas Boston*, vol. 3, George and Robert King, St. Nicholas Street, Aberdeen, 1848. https://books.google.com/books?id=CQFKAAAAMAAJ&pg=PA97&lpg=PA97&dq=#v=onepage&q&f=false.

Bucer, Martin. *Instruction in Christian Love*. Wipf and Stock, 2008. https://reformedbooksonline.com/topics/topics-by-subject/the-sincere-free-offer-of-the-gospel/historic-reformed-quotes-on-gods-revealed-will-as-his-desire-wish-and-pleasure/.

Bullinger, Heinrich, et al. *The First Helvetic Confession*. Basle, 1536. https://reformedbooksonline.com/topics/topics-by-subject/the-sincere-free-offer-of-the-gospel/the-first-helvetic-confession-1536-on-the-sincere-free-offer-of-the-gospel/.

Burroughs, Jeremiah. *Gospel Remission, Or a Treatise Shewing that True Blessedness Consists in Parton of Sin*. London, 1674.

Calvin, John. *The Harmony of the Gospels: Calvin's Commentary on Matthew, Mark, and Luke*. Electronic ed., Albany, Ages Software, 1998, Luke 19:41-44, par. 1. Logos.

---. *John*. Electronic ed., Albany, Ages Software, 1998, John 3:16, par. 1. Logos.

---. *2 Peter: Commentaries on the Catholic Epistles*. Electronic ed., Albany, Ages Software, 1998, 2 Pet. 3:9, par. 4. Logos.

---. *Secret Providence*. Article 7. https://calvinandcalvinism.wordpress.com/2007/11/03/god-desires-compliance-to-his-will-and-commands-as-standard-reformed-doctrine/.

*Canons of Dort*. Christian Reformed Church, 2011, PDF, Faith Alive Christian Resources, Approved by Synod 2011 of the Reformed Christian Church and by General Synod 2011 of the Reformed Church in America, Article 3, p. 126.

---. Article 5, p. 127.

Carson, D. A. *The Difficult Doctrine of the Love of God*. Wheaton, IL, Crossway Books, 2000. http://s3.amazonaws.com/tgc-documents/carson/2000_difficult_doctrine_of_the_love_of_god.pdf?utm_source=standfirm&utm_medium=post&utm_campaign=link.

Charnock, Stephen. "On the Goodness of God, Discourse 13." *The Existence and Attributes of God*, Baker, Grand Rapids, MI, 1996, pp. 285–287, https://reformedbooksonline.com/topics/topics-by-subject/the-sincere-free-offer-of-the-gospel/stephen-charnock-on-the-sincere-free-offer-of-the-gospel/.

Collinges, John. "Annotations on the Gospel of S. John", *A Commentary on the Holy Bible by Matthew Poole*, vol. 3, McLean, Virginia: MacDonald Publishing, 1990, pp. 777-778. http://calvinandcalvinism.com/?p=14721#more-14721.

Dekker, Harold. "God So Loved - ALL Men." *The Reformed Journal*, vol. 12, no. 11, Dec. 1962, pp. 5–7. http://theologicalmeditations.blogspot.com/2012/05/harold-dekker-1918-2006-on-divine-love.html.

Dickson, David, and James Durham. "Warrants and Motives to Believe." *The Sum of Saving Knowledge*, Johnstone, Hunter, & Co., Edinburgh, 1871. https://www.monergism.com/thethreshold/sdg/dickinson/dickson_sumsaving.html#chapter3.

Duncan, John "Rabbi". *In the Pulpit and at the Communion Table.* Edited by David Brown, Edinburgh: Edmonston and Douglas, 1874, 123-128. "Effectual Calling." The Westminster Presbyterian, par. 9.

Durham, James, and Don Kistler. "Gospel Presentations are the Strongest Invitations." *The Unsearchable Riches of Christ,* Soli Deo Gloria Publications, Morgan, PA, 2002, pp. 43-79, https://jamesdurham.wordpress.com/2007/07/28/weekly-update-13/.

Edwards, Jonathan. "Misery of the Damned", 1726, p. 3. *Works of Jonathan Edwards Online,* eds. Harry S. Stout, et al., Tony Byrne. https://reformedbooksonline.com/topics/topics-by-subject/the-sincere-free-offer-of-the-gospel/jonathan-edwards-on-the-sincere-free-offer-of-the-gospel/.

---. *Works of Jonathan Edwards.* "Concerning the Divine Decrees in General, and Election in Particular." Vol. 2, ch. 3, par. 2. http://www.ccel.org/e/edwards/works2.xi.iii.html.

Ellis, Jim. "Sufficient for All." The Highway, 2007, http://www.the-highway.com/sufficiency.html.

Flavel, John. *The Works of John Flavel.* "England's Duty Under the Present Gospel: Eleven Sermons on Revelation 3:20", vol. 4. https://reformedbooksonline.com/topics/topics-by-subject/the-sincere-free-offer-of-the-gospel/john-flavel-on-the-sincere-free-offer-of-the-gospel/.

Fuller, Andrew. *The Gospel Worthy of All Accepta-tion.* "Antinomianism and the Righteousness of the Law," Biographia Evangelica, George M. Ella. http://evangelica.de/articles/doctrine/antinomianismand-the-righteousness-of-the-law/.

Henry, Matthew. *Commentary on the Whole Bible.* Hendrickson Publishers, Inc., 1991.

---. *Matthew Henry Concise Bible Commentary.* 1 John 4:7, Sacred-texts.com. http://www.sacred-texts.com/bib/cmt/mhcc/jo1004.htm.

---. *Matthew Henry Concise Bible Commentary.* Rev. 22:17, Bibletools.info. http://bibletools.info/reference/Rev_22.17.

Horton, Michael. "Reformed Theology Vs. Hyper-Calvinism." Ligonier Ministries, par. 6. Tabletalk Magazine, 2005.

Hulse, Erroll. "The Love of God for All Mankind," *Reformation Today,* Nov–Dec 1983. http://www.gty.org/resources/Questions/QA193.

---. "The Example of the English Puritans." *Reformation Today,* 153, Sept/Oct 1996. http://theologicalmeditations.blogspot.com/2009/06/erroll-hulse-on-john-316-and-hyper.html.

---. "John 3:16 and Hyper-Calvinism," *Reformation Today,* 135, September-October, 1993, 27-30. http://theologicalmeditations.blogspot.com/2009/06/erroll-hulse-on-john-316-and-hyper.html.

Kuiper, R.B. *For Whom Did Christ Die?* Wipf and Stock Publishers, Eugene, OR, 2003, p. 86. http://theologicalmeditations.blogspot.com/2006/09/r-b-kuiper-quote.html.

*London Baptist Confession of Faith.* Chapter 7, 1677/89. http://www.ccel.org/ccel/anonymous/bcf.ii.viii.html.

Luther, Martin. *Bondage of the Will.* Translated by J.I. Packer & O.R. Johnston, Fleming H. Revell, 1957.

Manton, Thomas. Volume 2, Sermon 16 on John 3:16, David Ponter, p. 340-2. https://reformedbooksonline.com/topics/topics-by-subject/the-sincere-free-offer-of-the-gospel/thomas-manton-on-the-sincere-free-offer-of-the-gospel/.

McCheyne, Robert Murray, and Andrew A. Bonar. *Memoirs and Remains of the Rev. Robert Murray McCheyne.* Oliphant Anderson & Ferrier, 1894, p. 325. Logos.

Murray, John. "The Free Offer of the Gospel." https://reformedbooksonline.com/murray-and-the-post-reformation-compared-on-the-sincere-free-offer-of-the-gospel/.

Packer, J.I. *Celebrating the Saving Work of God.* Carlisle, Paternoster Press, 1998.

Perkins, William. *A Treatise of God's Free Grace, and Man's Free Will.* Cambridge, 1601, pp. 44-47. http://calvinand-calvinism.com/?p=5219.

Pink, Arthur W. "Objections to God's Sovereignty Answered." *The Highway,* http://www.the-highway.com/objsovereignty_Pink.html.

Rutherford, Samuel. *The Trial and Triumph of Faith.* 1845, 302-303. https://reformedbooksonline.com/topics/topics-by-subject/the-sincere-free-offer-of-the-gospel/samuel-rutherford-on-the-sincere-free-offer-of-the-gospel/.

Ryle, J.C. *Ryle's Expository Thoughts on the Gospels.* Vol. 3, Grand Rapids, MI, Zondervan, 1977.

---. *An Estimate of Manton by JC Ryle in 1870.* Tony Byrne. https://reformedbooksonline.com/topics/topics-by-subject/the-sincere-free-offer-of-the-gospel/thomas-manton-on-the-sincere-free-offer-of-the-gospel/.

Shedd, W.G.T. *Calvinism: Pure and Mixed.* New York: Scribner's, 1893, p. 28-29. Internet Archive, Princeton Theological Seminary Library, https://archive.org/details/calvinismpuremix00shed.

Sproul, R.C. "Abundant Love." Ligonier Ministries, pars. 8, 15, 16. Tabletalk Magazine, 2004.

Spurgeon, Charles. "The Silver Trumpet." Preached on March 24, 1861 from the text of Isaiah 1:18. http://www.examiningcalvinism.com/files/Complaints/Charge_Invitations.html.

---. "Sovereign Grace and Man's Responsibility." New Park Street Pulpit, vol. 4, 1858, 341.

Waldron, Samuel E. *Modern Exposition of the 1689 Baptist Confession of Faith.* Durham, England, Evangelical Press, 1989.

Watson, Thomas. *A Body of Divinity.* Christian Classics Ethereal Library, Grand Rapids, MI, 1686, 166. http://www.ccel.org/w/Watson/divinity/cache/divinity.pdf.

# ABOUT THE AUTHORS

Trevor Johnson,
Missionary and Author

Trevor and Teresa have been married for 17 years. They serve and love a remote tribal group in Papua, Indonesia.

They are both registered nurses and Trevor is an ordained Christian minister. They are deeply aware that all they have and are is by the grace of God, and that any blessings they receive are to be used to bless others. They mean to live their lives in gratitude to a Savior who loves them and gave Himself for them. Confronted by the pains and evils of the world, they desire not to shrink back or shield their eyes, but instead to face the hurts and struggles of others, being like Christ to those who need His love despite their own shortcomings, and to bless others on their journey through life.

Trevor and Teresa have four wonderful children (Noah, 12; Alethea, 9; Perpetua, 5; and Baby Gideon) and two more waiting for them in heaven. They pray their children will grow up as gentle, loving souls who will work for a better world and not merely live for their own comfort and ease.

Trevor and Teresa believe in a sovereign God who weaves all of our lives together for His greater glory.

"Resolved, to live with all my might, while I do live."

~ Jonathan Edwards' Resolutions

"I sought the Lord, and afterward I knew he moved my soul to seek him, seeking me; it was not I that found, O Savior true; no, I was found of thee.

Thou didst reach forth thy hand and mine enfold; I walked and sank not on the storm-vexed sea; 'twas not so much that I on thee took hold, as thou, dear Lord, on me.

I find, I walk, I love, but oh, the whole of love is but my answer, Lord, to thee; for thou wert long beforehand with my soul, always thou lovedst me."

~ Anonymous

## Grace Rankin,
## Contributor and Editor

Grace is a Christian author, freelance writer, and editor serving the Lord in Indiana.

She earned her Bachelor's Degree in English from Thomas Edison State University, and uses her love of writing to help others and be a light for Christ.

Grace is passionate about the gospel of Jesus and desires to use her career as a writer to share His love with the world, starting with her freelance business Writing Life, and eventually in her published works.

She lives in Indiana with her family and enjoys playing the piano, hiking, and reading.

Because of Christ,

> "The blind receive sight and the lame walk, the lepers are cleansed and the deaf hear, the dead are raised up, and the poor have the gospel preached to them."

~ Matthew 11:5 ~

> "Come to Me, all who are weary and heavy-laden, and I will give you rest. Take My yoke upon you and learn from Me, for I am gentle and humble in heart, and you will find rest for your souls."

~ Matthew 11:28-29 ~